Steel Guitar Zone.com

Maximum Success Music Instruction

Pedal Steel Guitar Player's

TAB Notebook

By Joe Stoebenau

The Pedal Steel Fretboard

The charts below diagram the fretboard of the
E9 and C6 necks on the conventional 10 string double neck Pedal steel guitar.
They can be used as a handy reference for the notes on the pedal steel guitar.

E9

1	F#	G	G#/Ab	A	A#/Bb	B	C	C#/Db	D	D#/Eb	E	F	F#/Gb
2	D#	E	F	F#/Gb	G	G#/Ab	A	A#/Bb	B	C	C#/Db	D	D#/Eb
3	G#	A	A#/Bb	B	C	C#/Db	D	D#/Eb	E	F	F#/Gb	G	G#/Ab
4	E	F	F#/Gb	G	G#/Ab	A	A#/Bb	B	C	C#/Db	D	D#/Eb	E
5	B	C	C#/Db	D	D#/Eb	E	F	F#/Gb	G	G#/Ab	A	A#/Bb	B
6	G#	A	A#/Bb	B	C	C#/Db	D	D#/Eb	E	F	F#/Gb	G	G#/Ab
7	F#	G	G#/Ab	A	A#/Bb	B	C	C#/Db	D	D#/Eb	E	F	F#/Gb
8	E	F	F#/Gb	G	G#/Ab	A	A#/Bb	B	C	C#/Db	D	D#/Eb	E
9	D	D#/Eb	E	F	F#/Gb	G	G#/Ab	A	A#/Bb	B	C	C#/Db	D
10	B	C	C#/Db	D	D#/Eb	E	F	F#/Gb	G	G#/Ab	A	A#/Bb	B

C6

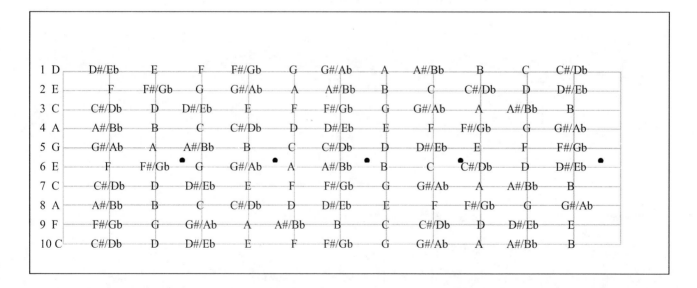

1	D	D#/Eb	E	F	F#/Gb	G	G#/Ab	A	A#/Bb	B	C	C#/Db	
2	E	F	F#/Gb	G	G#/Ab	A	A#/Bb	B	C	C#/Db	D	D#/Eb	
3	C	C#/Db	D	D#/Eb	E	F	F#/Gb	G	G#/Ab	A	A#/Bb	B	
4	A	A#/Bb	B	C	C#/Db	D	D#/Eb	E	F	F#/Gb	G	G#/Ab	
5	G	G#/Ab	A	A#/Bb	B	C	C#/Db	D	D#/Eb	E	F	F#/Gb	
6	E	F	F#/Gb	G	G#/Ab	A	A#/Bb	B	C	C#/Db	D	D#/Eb	
7	C	C#/Db	D	D#/Eb	E	F	F#/Gb	G	G#/Ab	A	A#/Bb	B	
8	A	A#/Bb	B	C	C#/Db	D	D#/Eb	E	F	F#/Gb	G	G#/Ab	
9	F	F#/Gb	G	G#/Ab	A	A#/Bb	B	C	C#/Db	D	D#/Eb	E	
10	C	C#/Db	D	D#/Eb	E	F	F#/Gb	G	G#/Ab	A	A#/Bb	B	

Standard Pedal Steel Tuning Charts

E9

String	Note	Left Knee L	Left Knee R	Pedal A	Pedal B	Pedal C	Right Knee L	Right Knee R
1	F#						G	
2	D#							D
3	G#				A			
4	E	F	Eb			F#		
5	B			C#		C#		
6	G#				A			
7	F#						G	
8	E	F	Eb					
9	D							C#
10	B			C#				

C6

String	Note	Pedal 4	Pedal 5	Pedal 6	Pedal 7	Pedal 8	F knee	G knee	H knee	I knee
1	D					D#				
2	E			F						
3	C				D		B	C#		
4	A	B			B				Ab	Bb
5	G		F#							
6	E			Eb						
7	C					C#				
8	A	B								
9	F		F#			E				
10	C		D			A				

How To Read Pedal Steel Guitar Tablature

Tablature, is a system of notation that tells the guitar player where to place the *steel* on the strings. (The steel is the metal bar used to play the pedal steel guitar).
Tablature is read from the left side of the page to the right and has ten lines representing the ten strings on the pedal steel guitar.

The top line represents the first string and they are numbered down to the lowest line which represents the tenth string.

Numbers are placed on the lines to represent what fret to play a particular string.
The pedals are diagrammed by placing letters next to the fret number as can be seen in the diagram below.

The diagonal lines indicate a slide with the *steel* up from one note to the next.

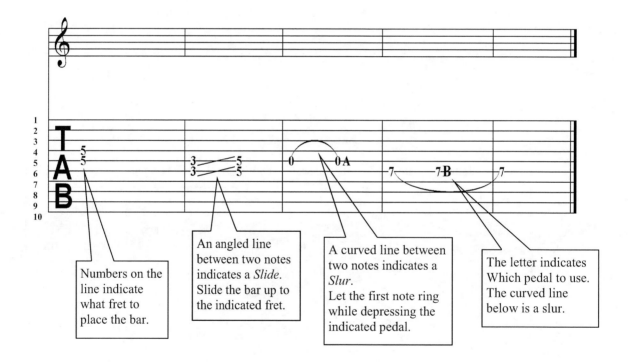

Numbers on the line indicate what fret to place the bar.

An angled line between two notes indicates a *Slide*. Slide the bar up to the indicated fret.

A curved line between two notes indicates a *Slur*. Let the first note ring while depressing the indicated pedal.

The letter indicates Which pedal to use. The curved line below is a slur.

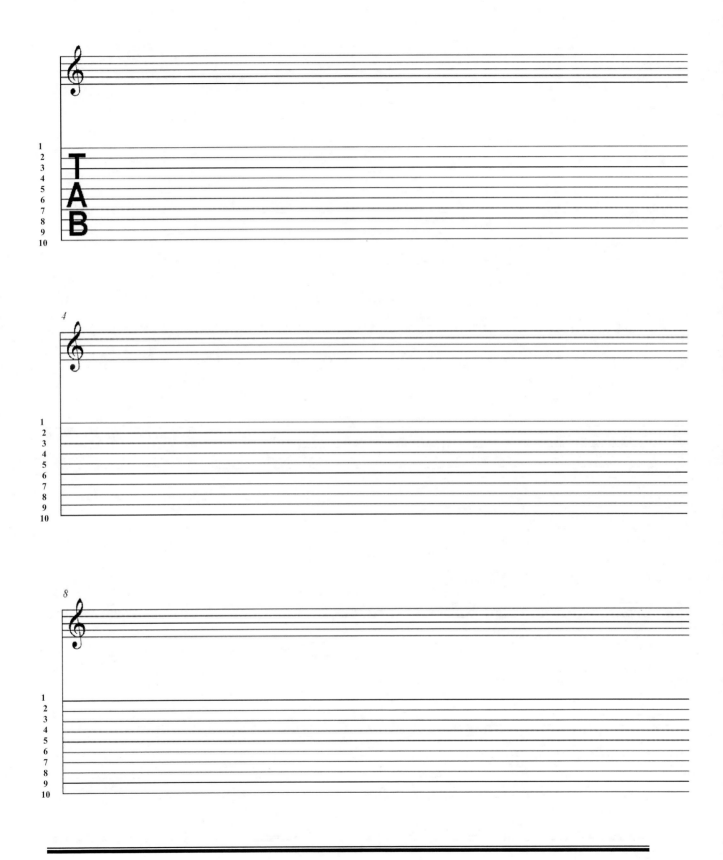

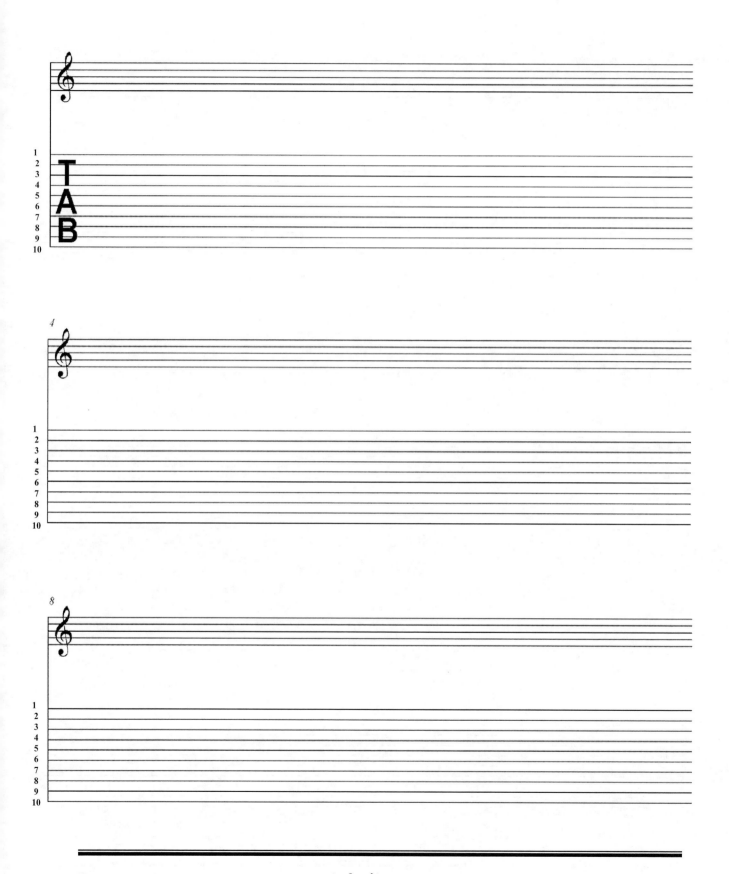

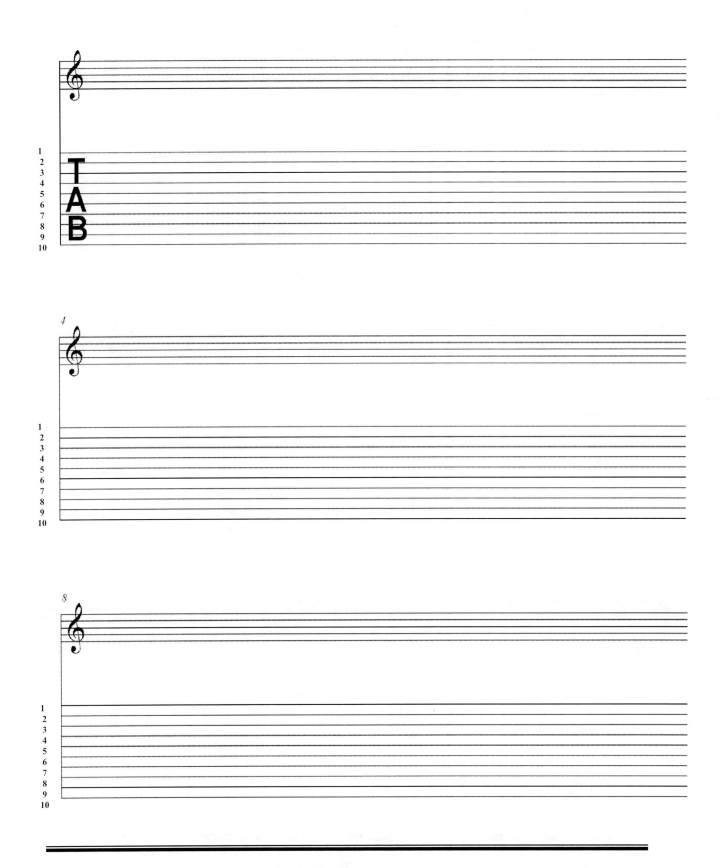

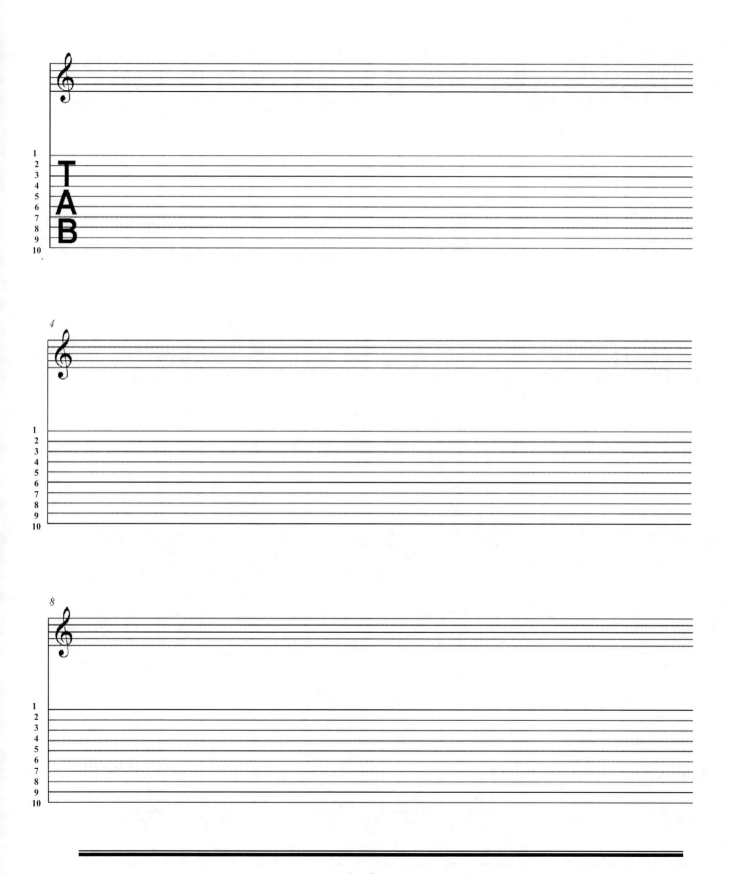

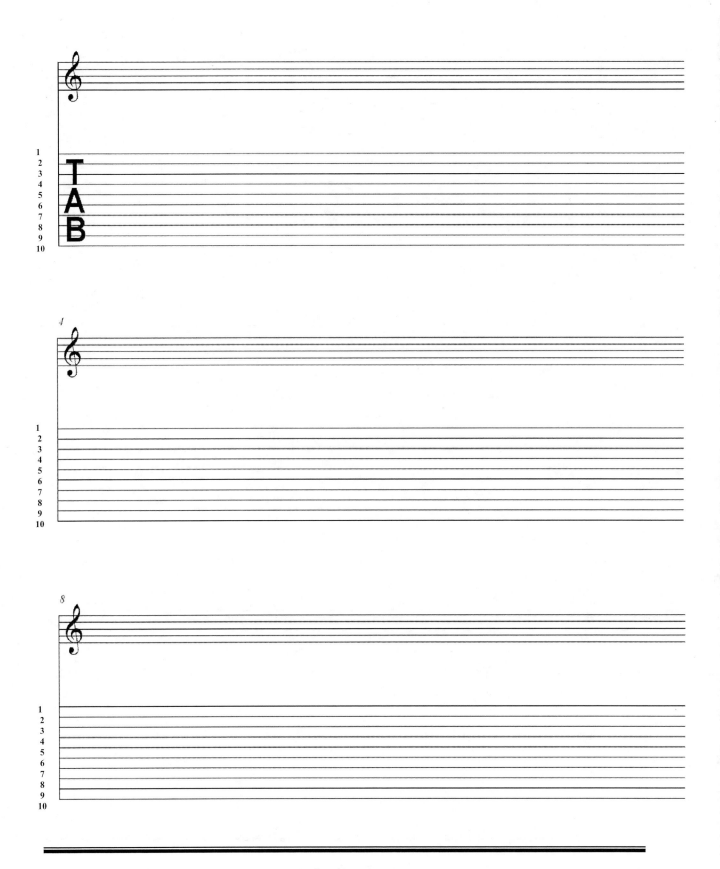

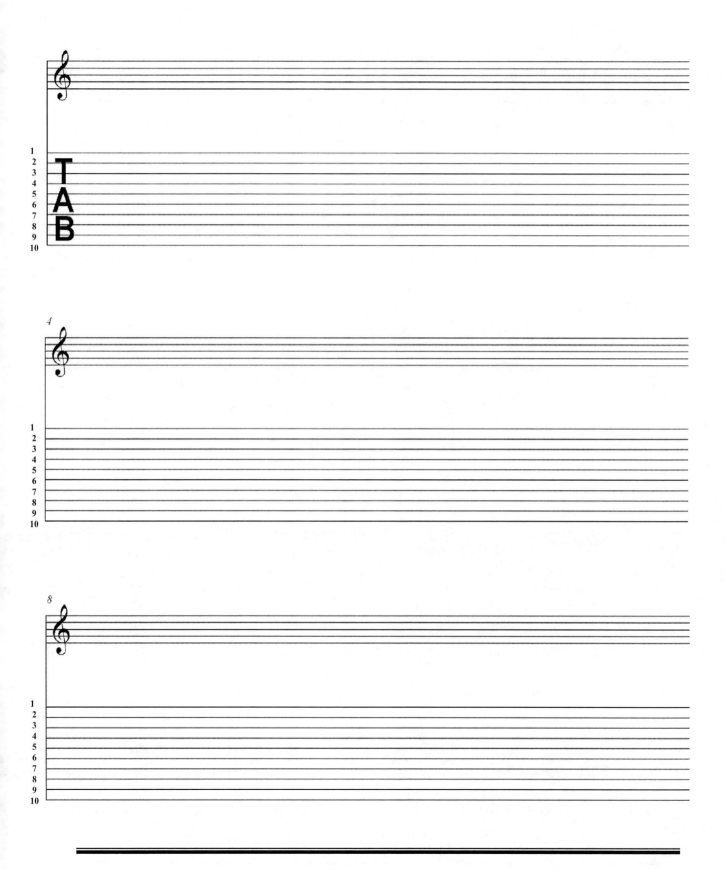

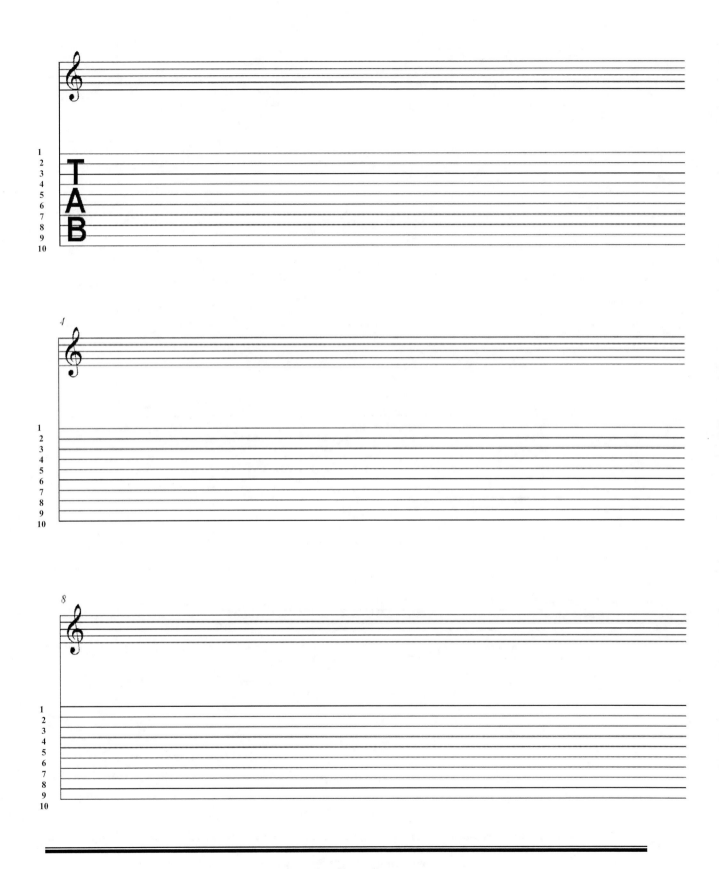

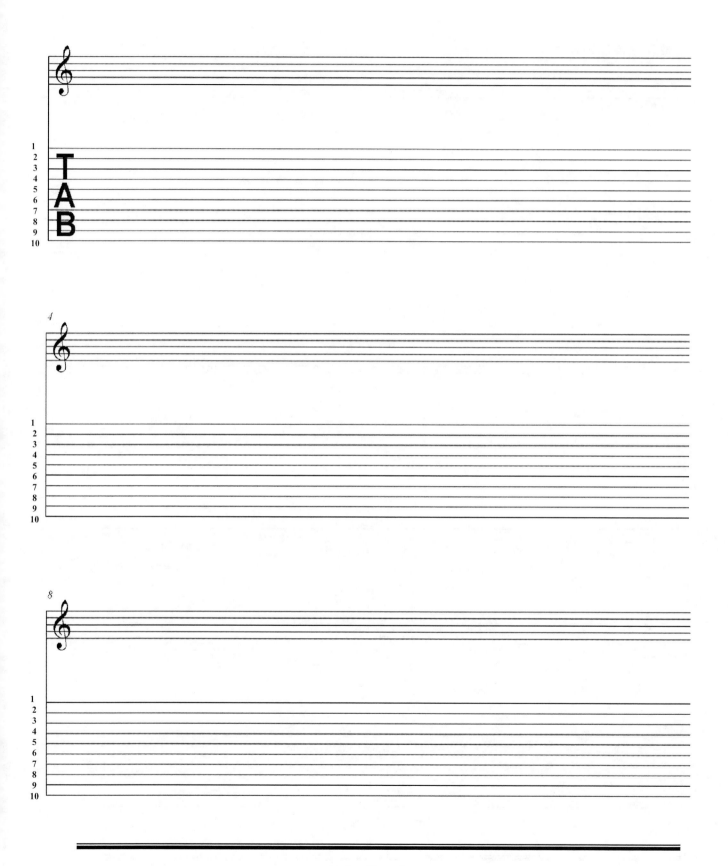

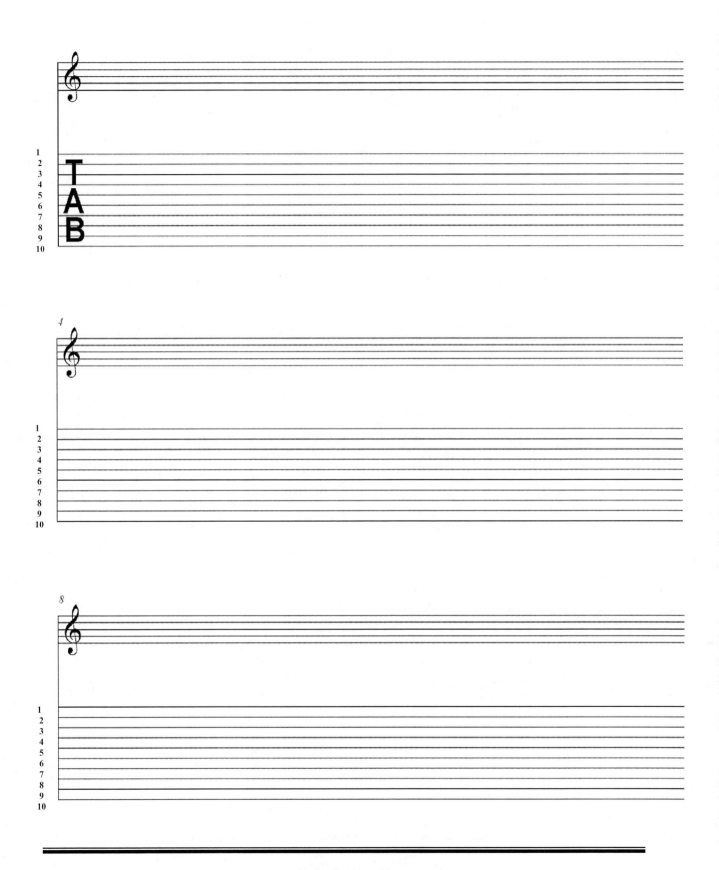

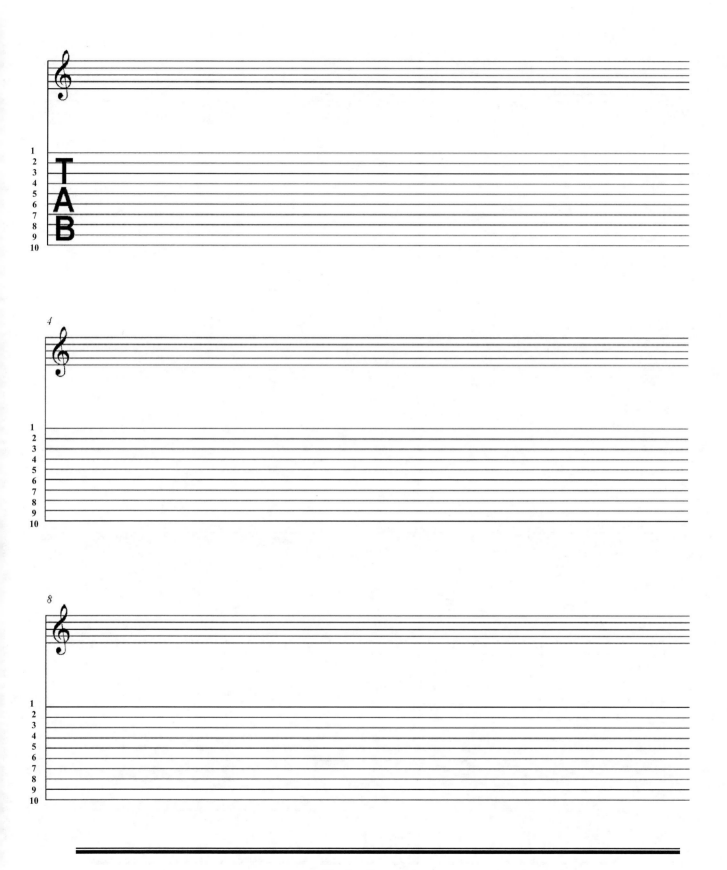

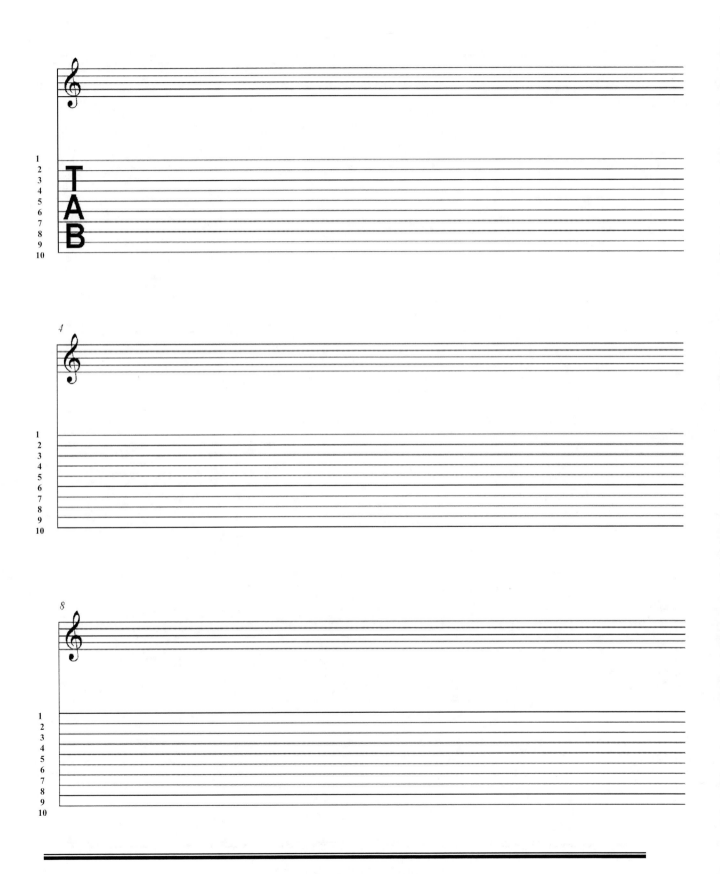

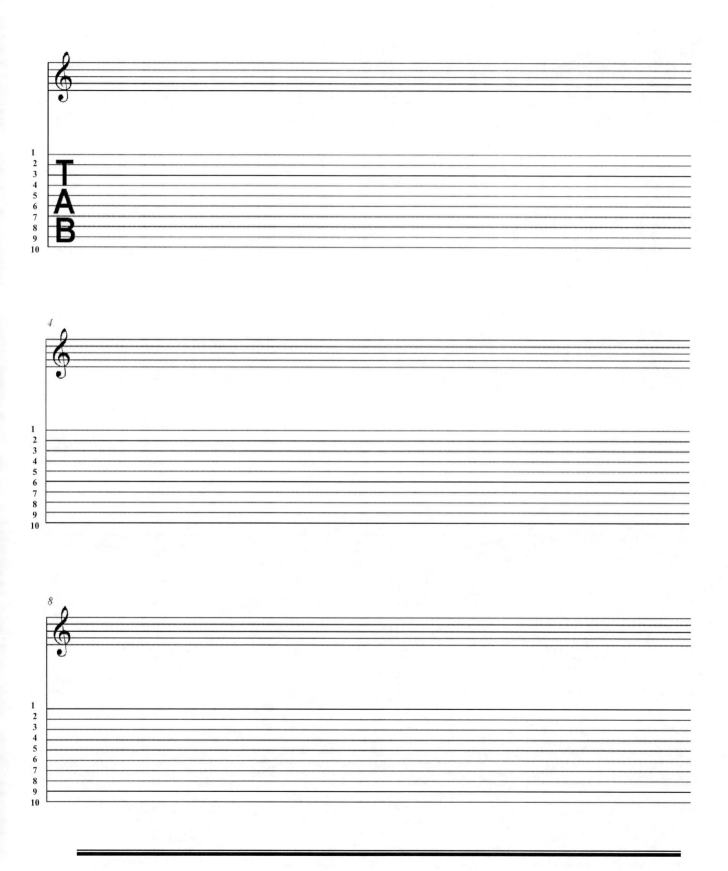

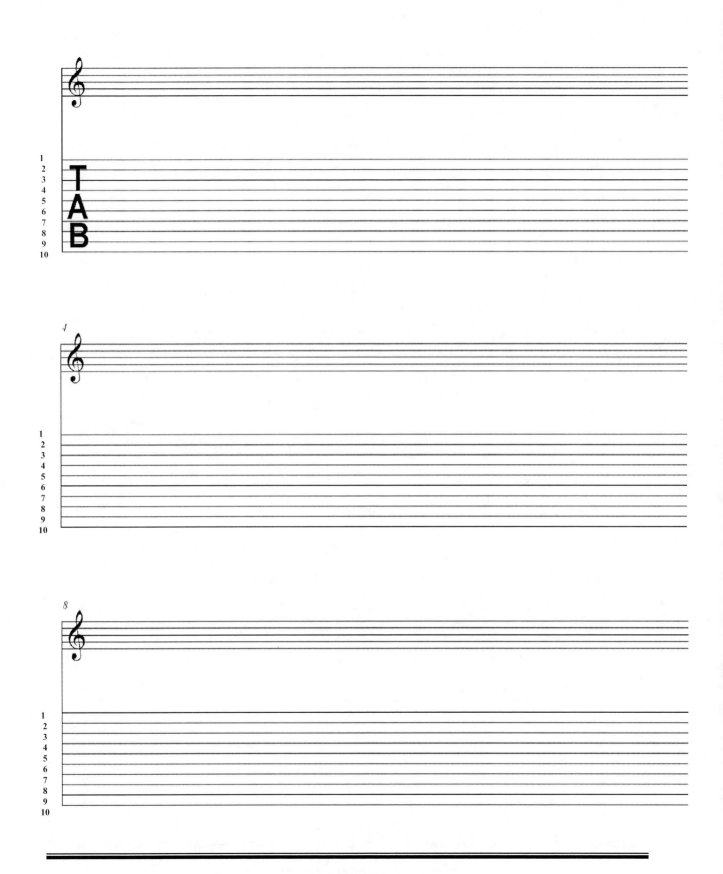

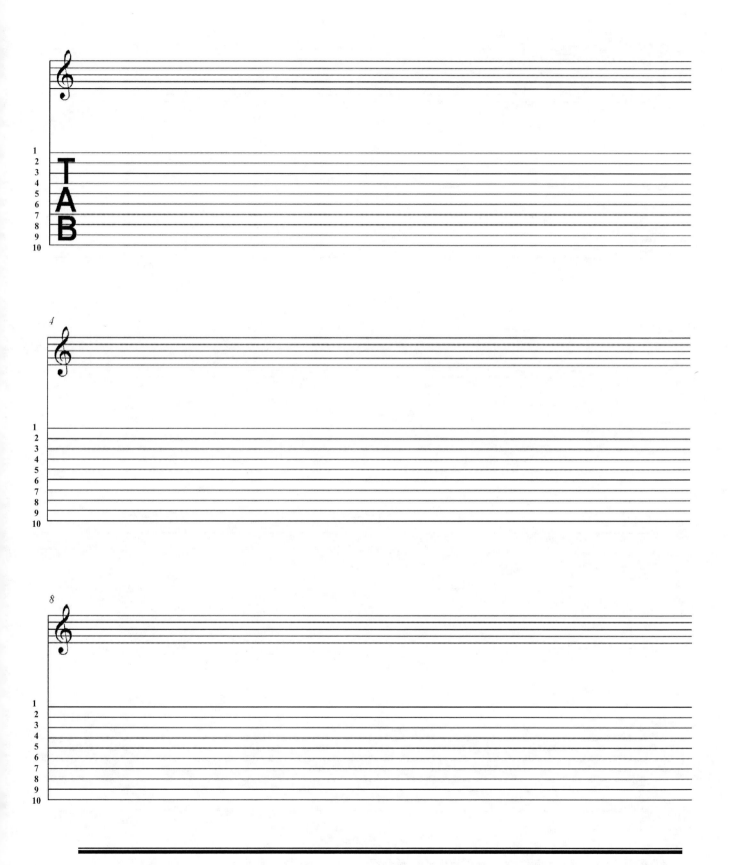

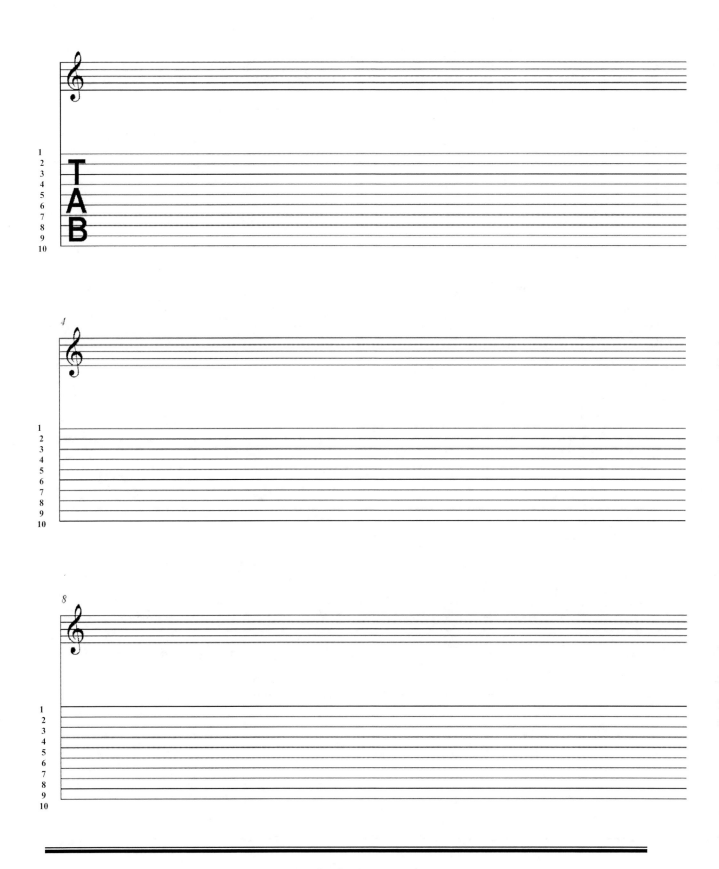

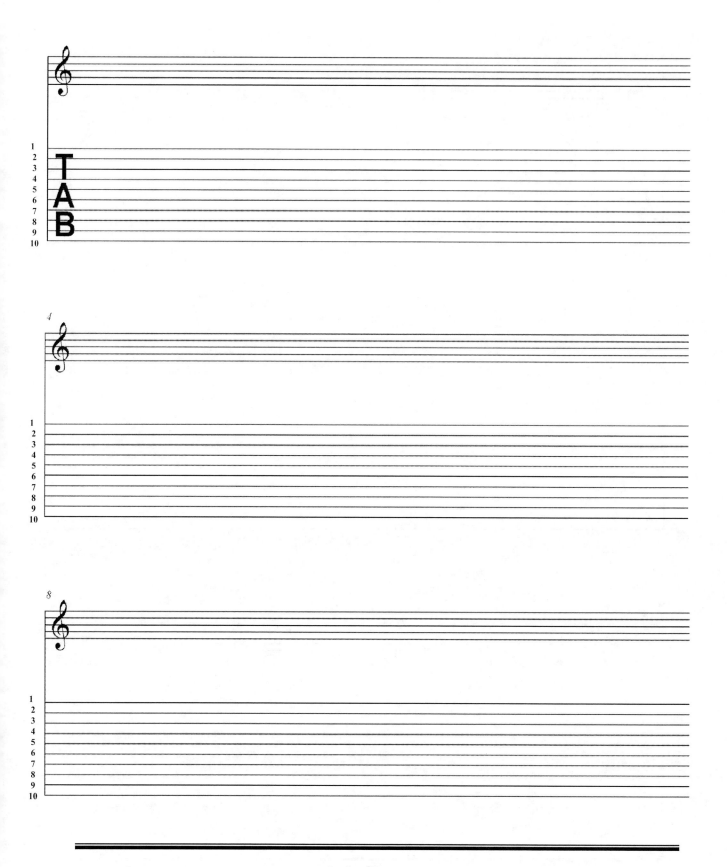

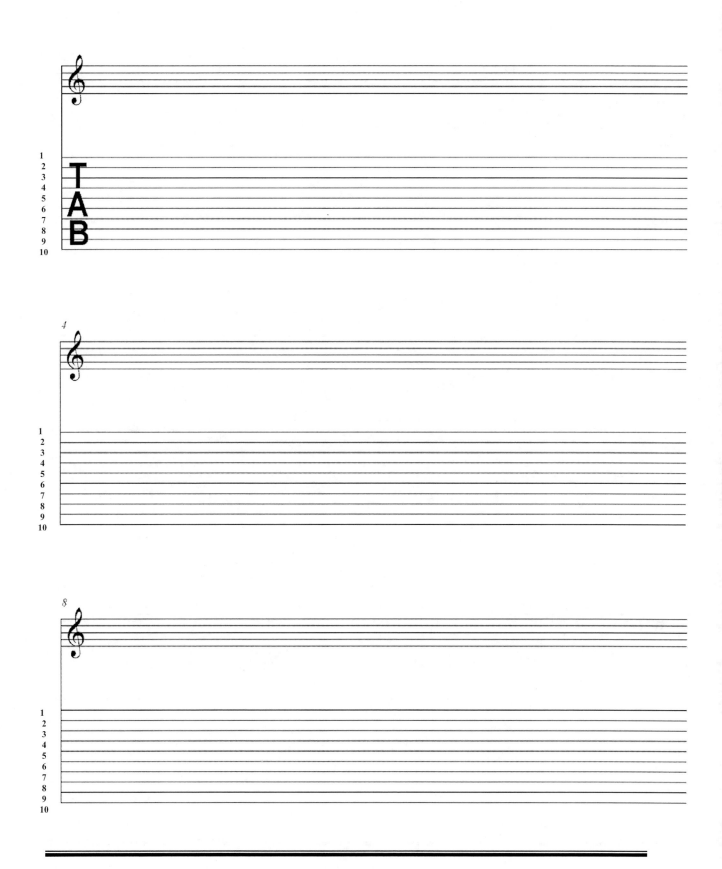

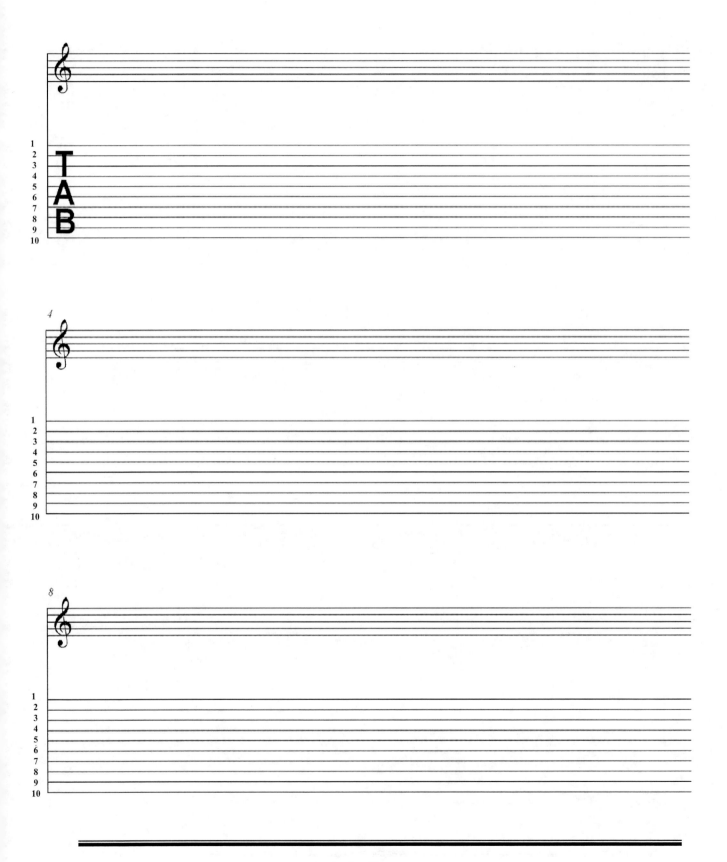

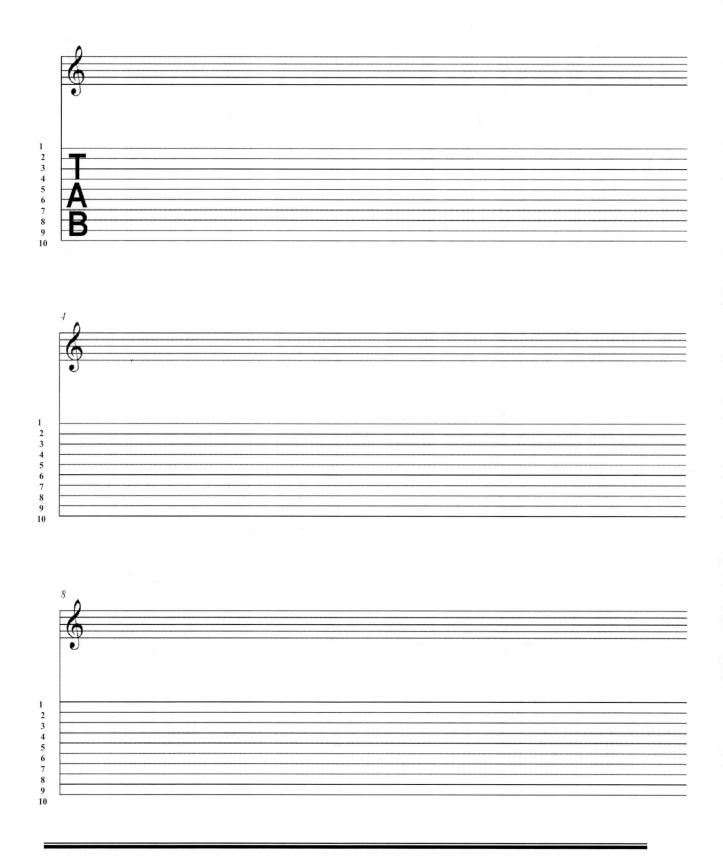

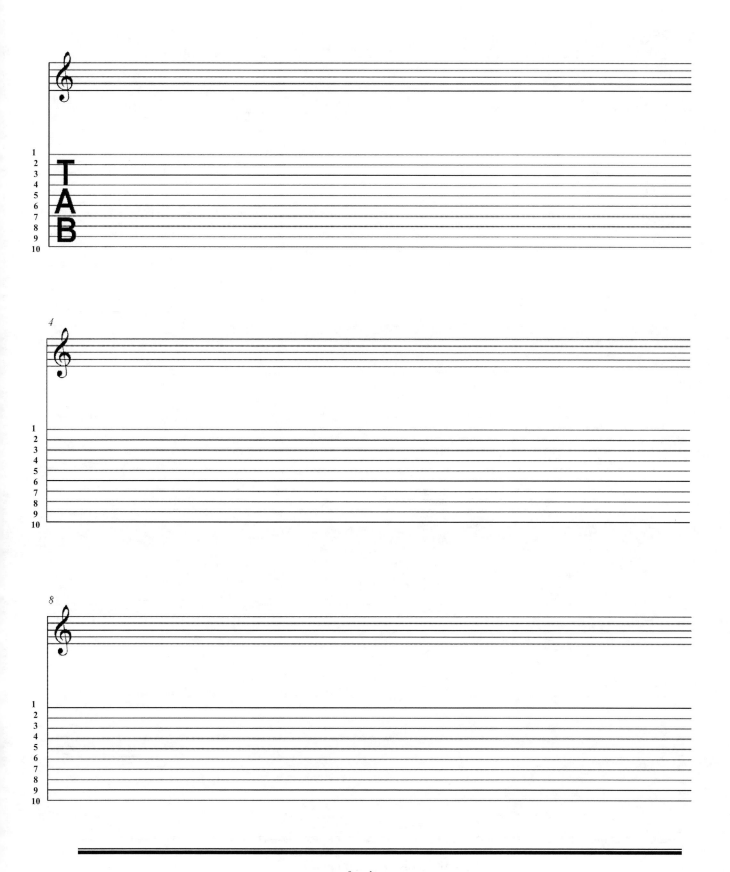

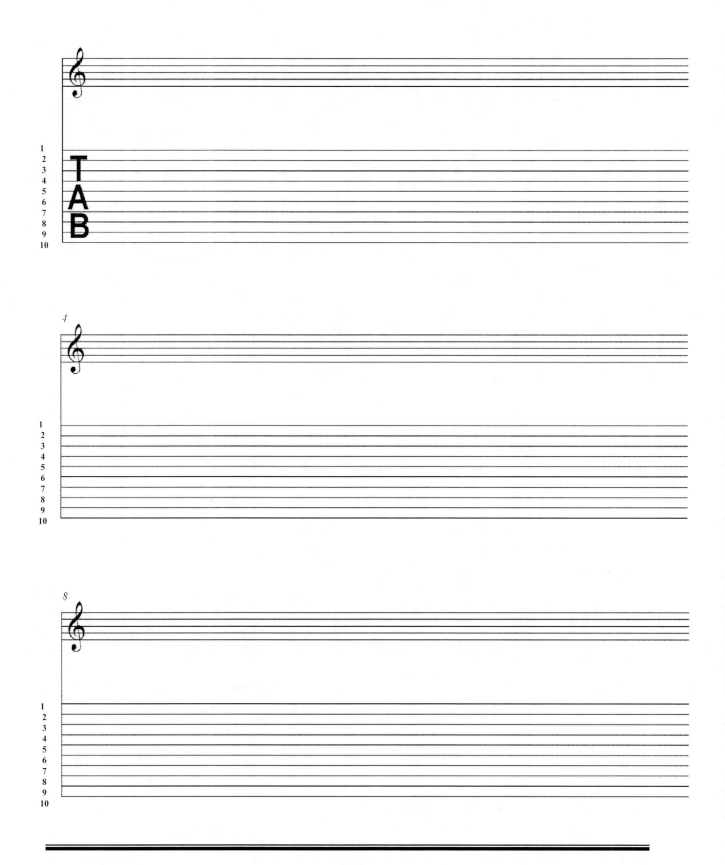

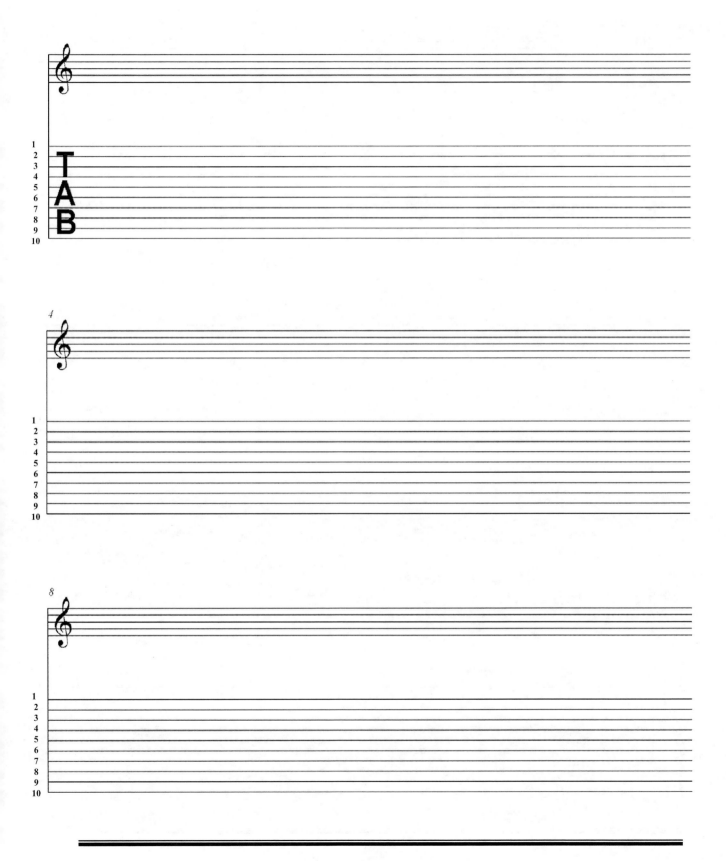

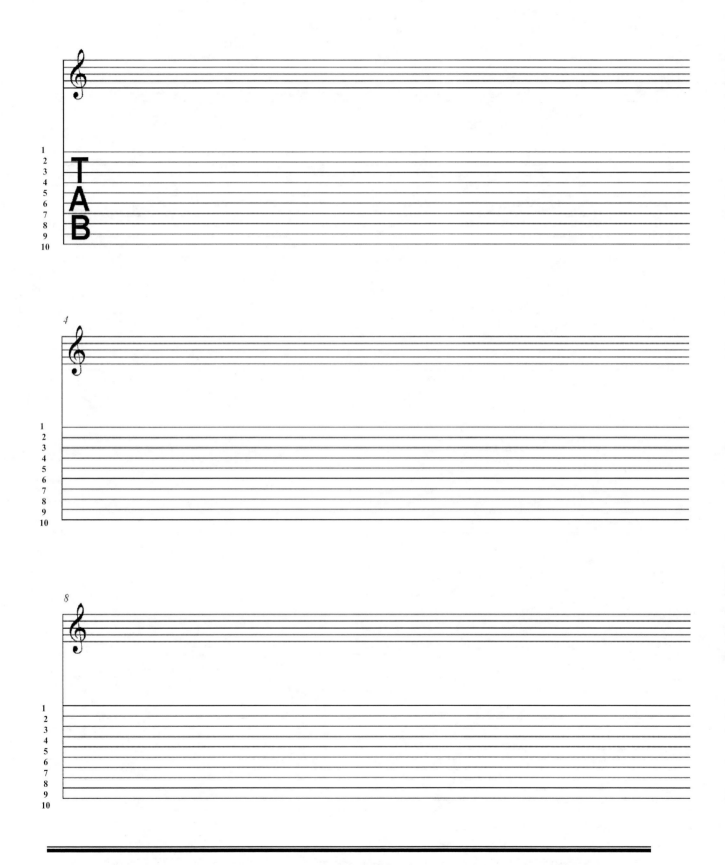

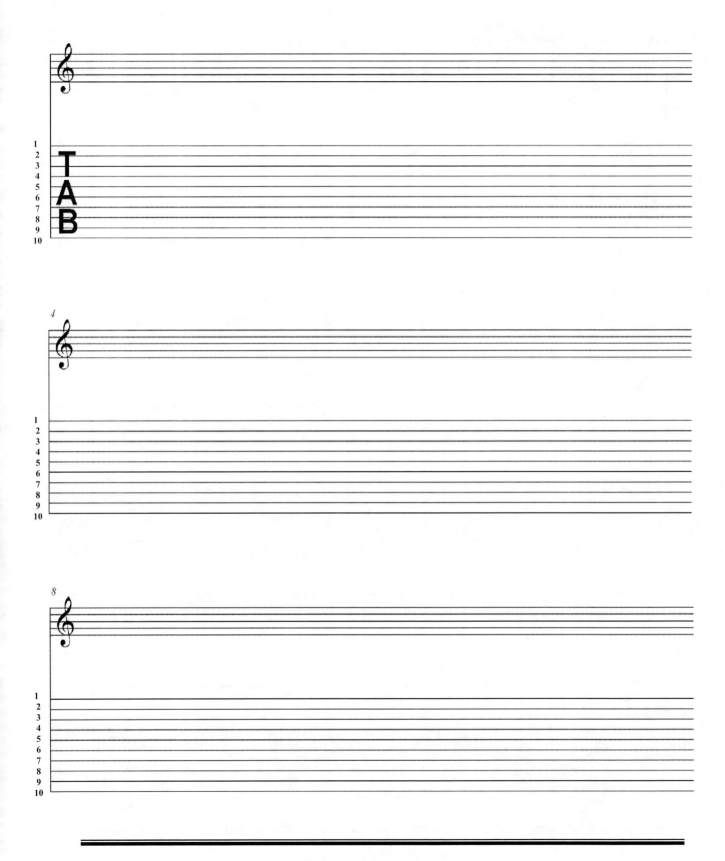

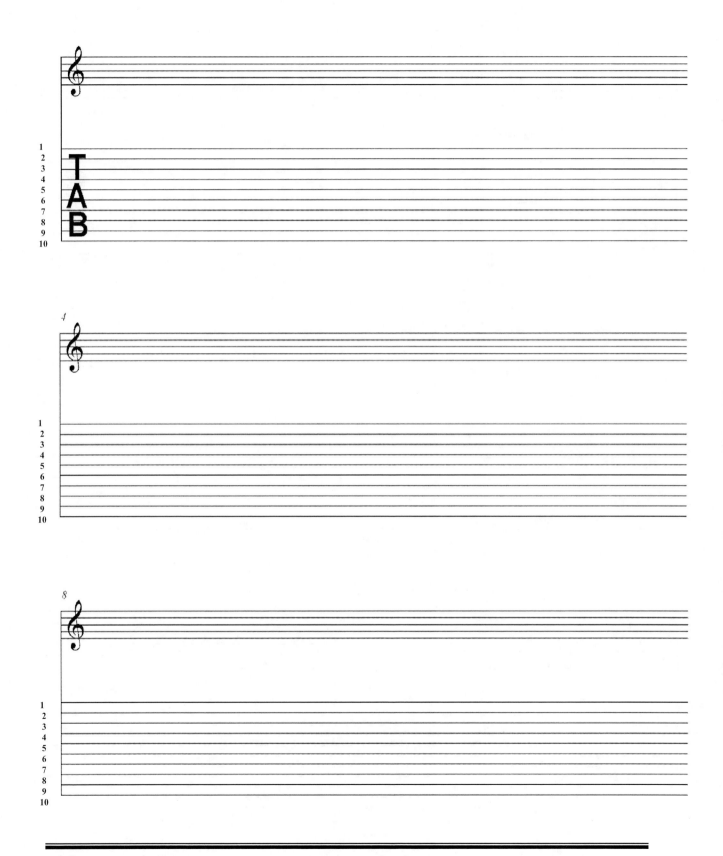

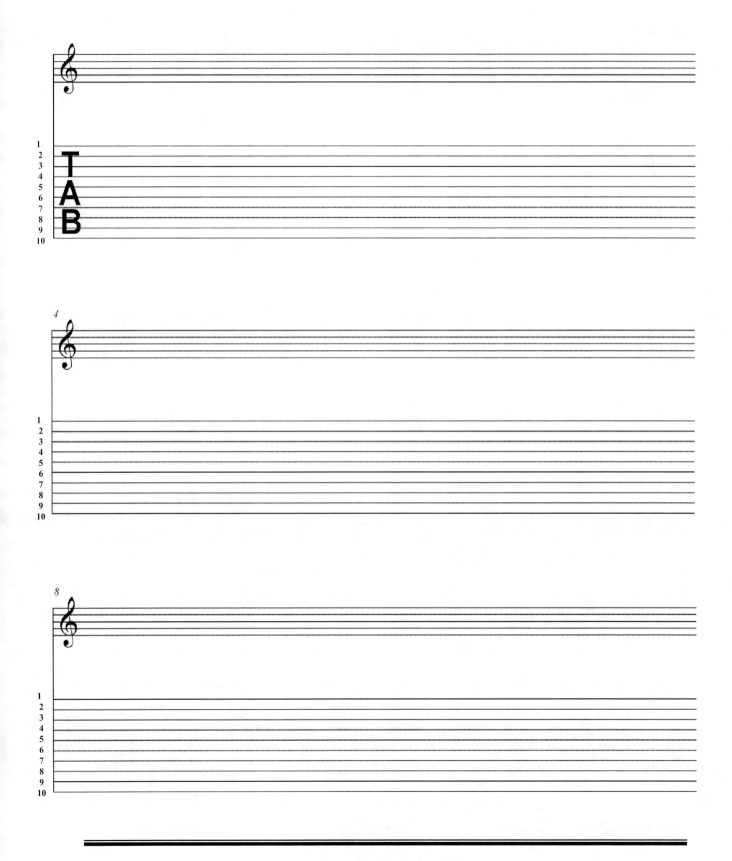

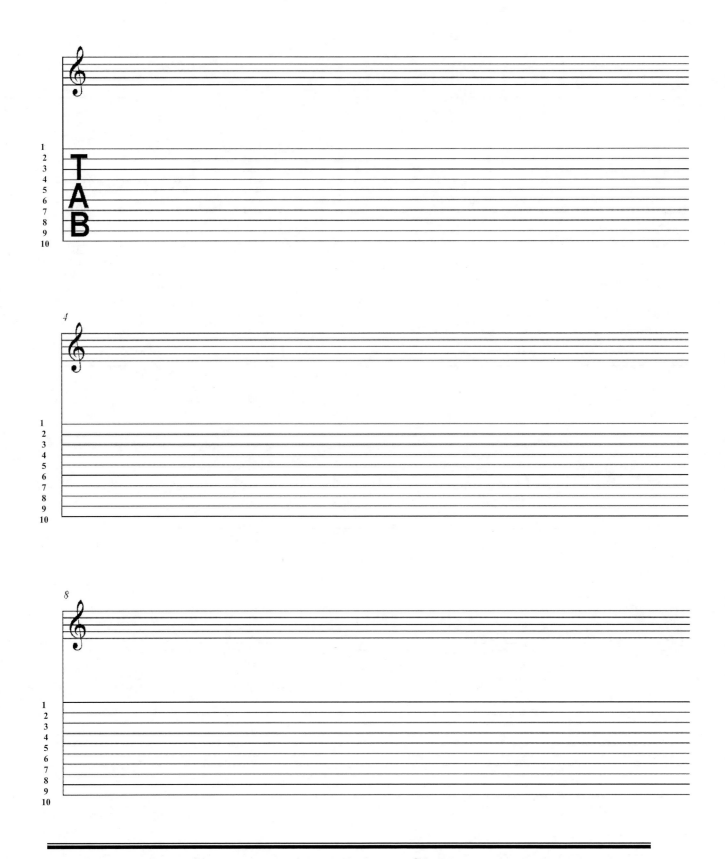

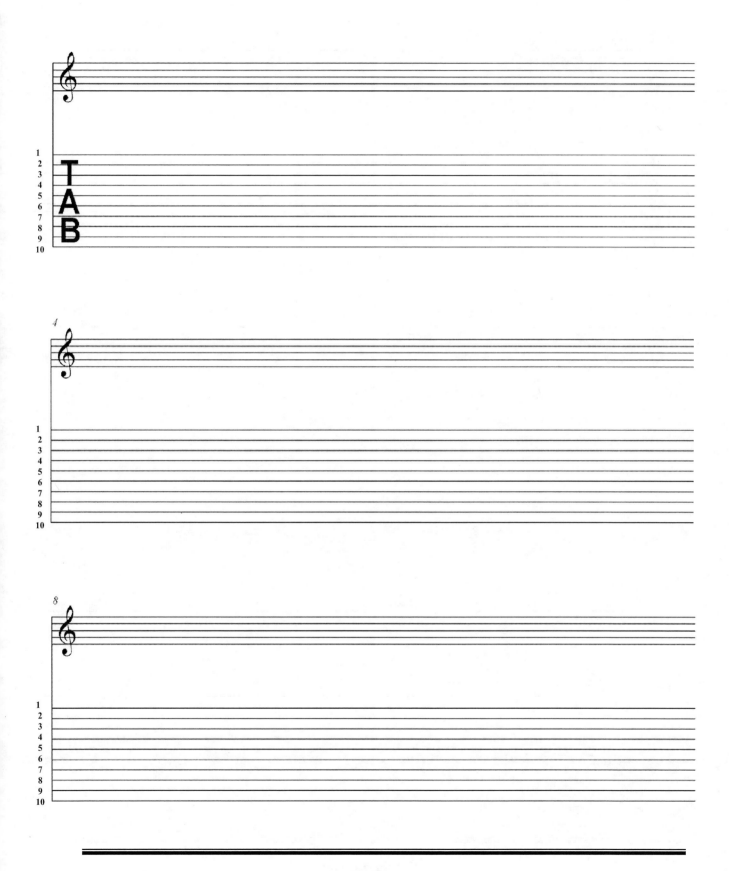

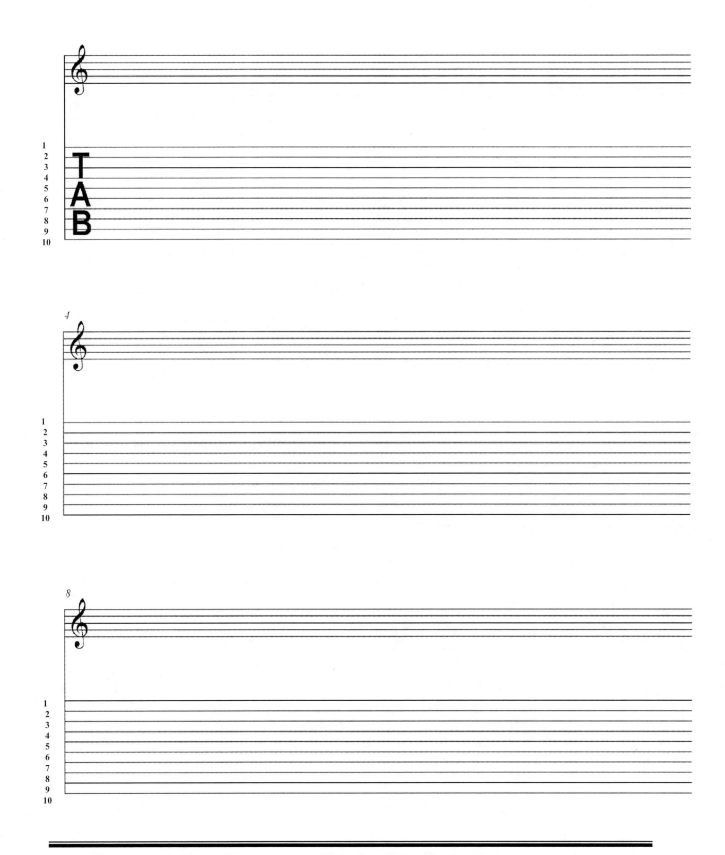

www.steelguitarzone.com

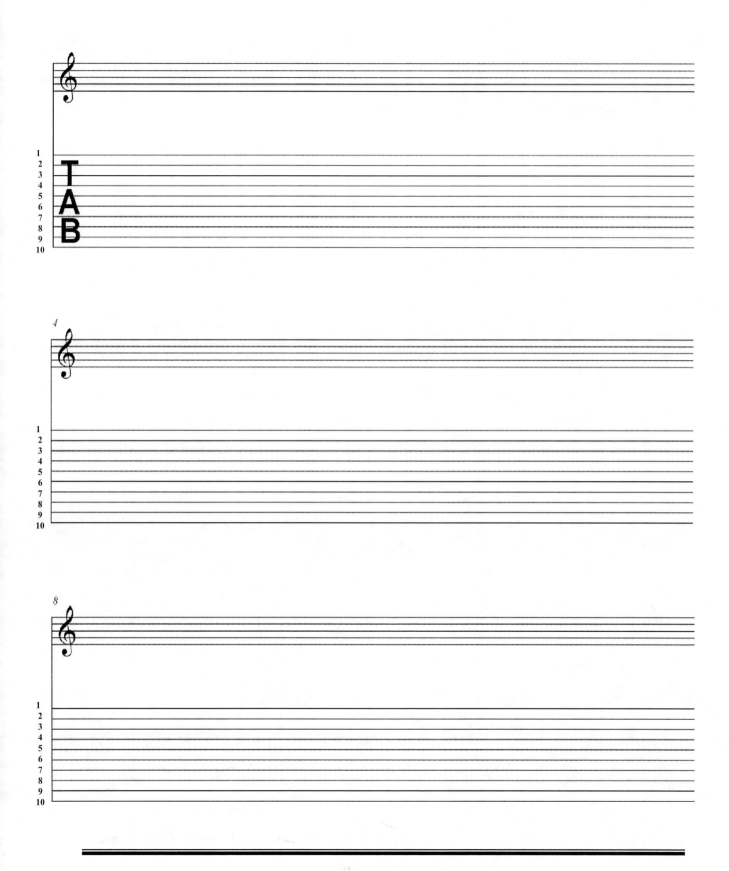

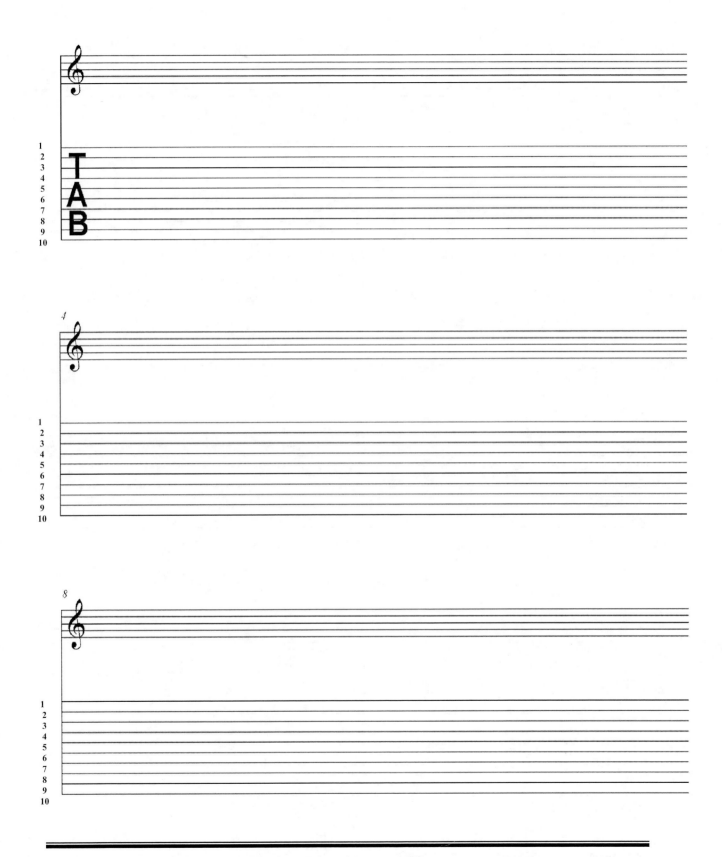

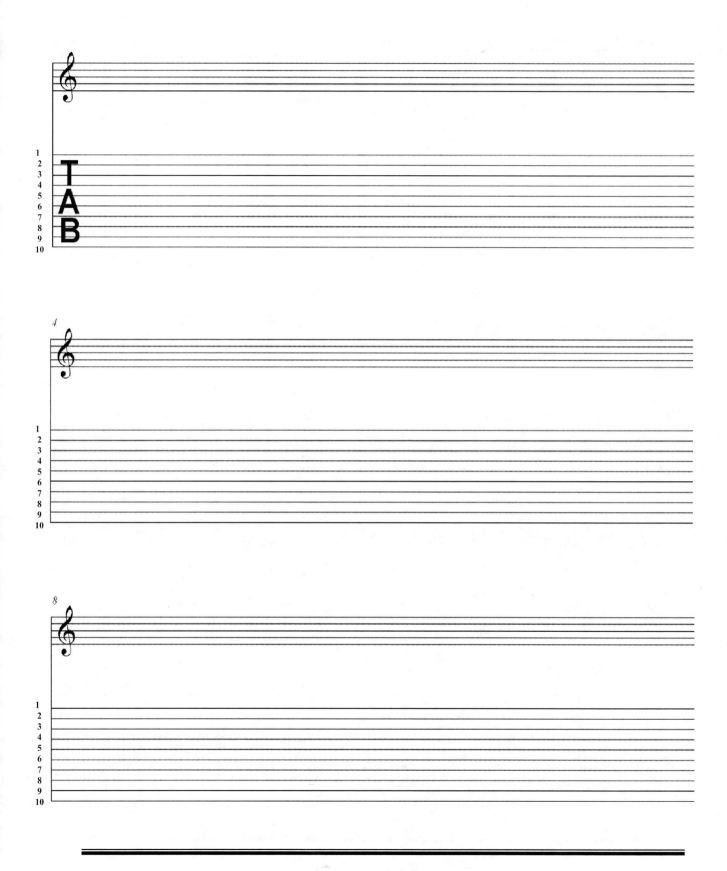

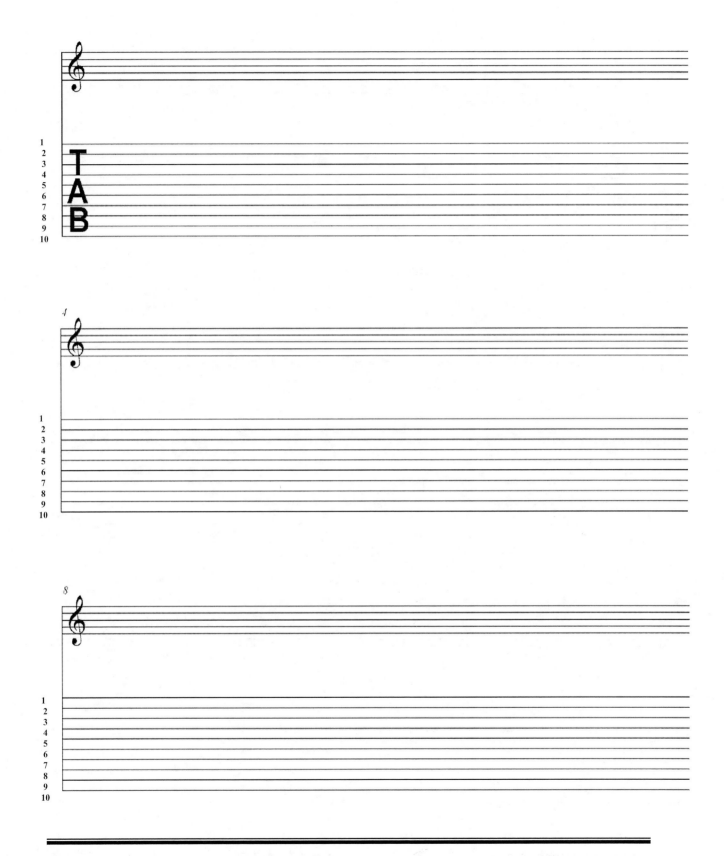

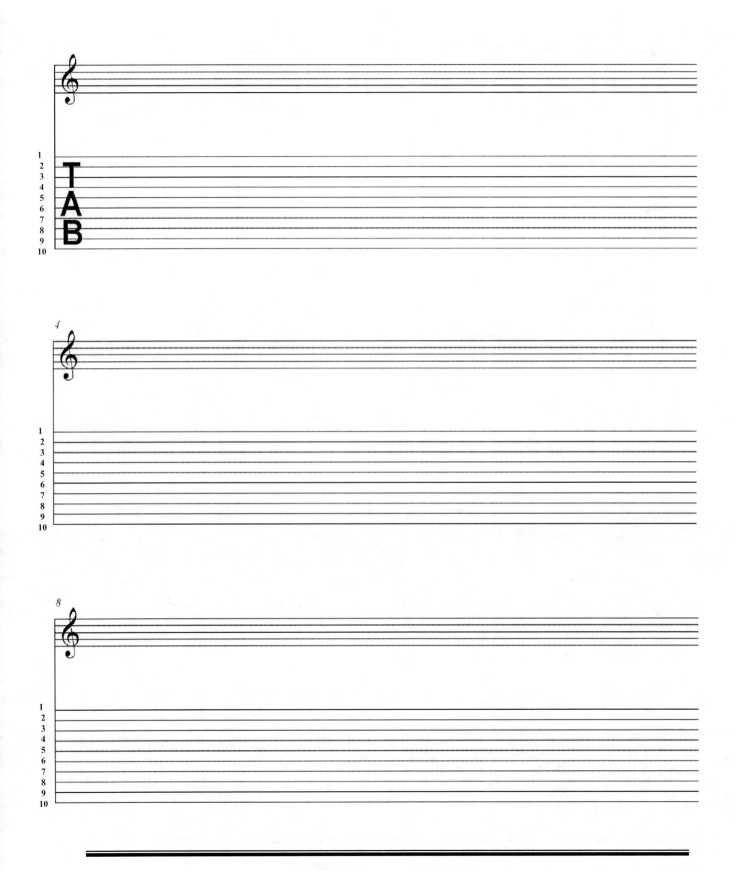

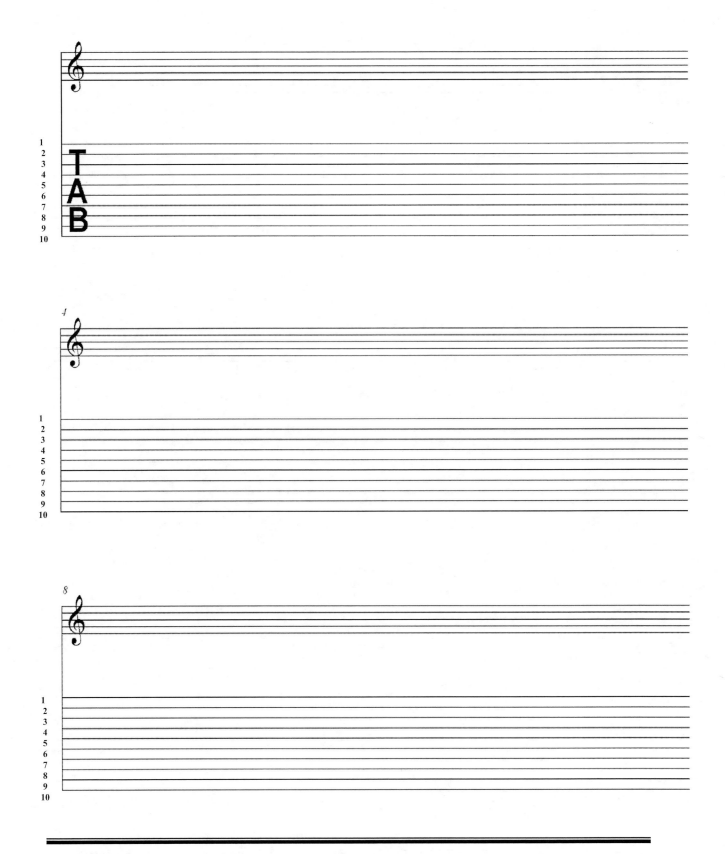

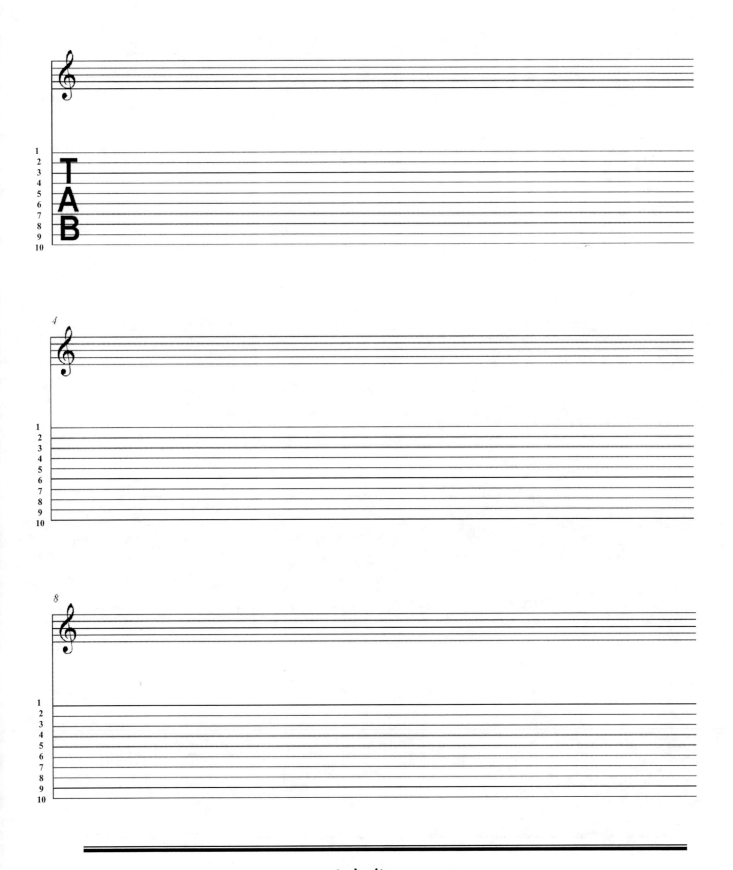

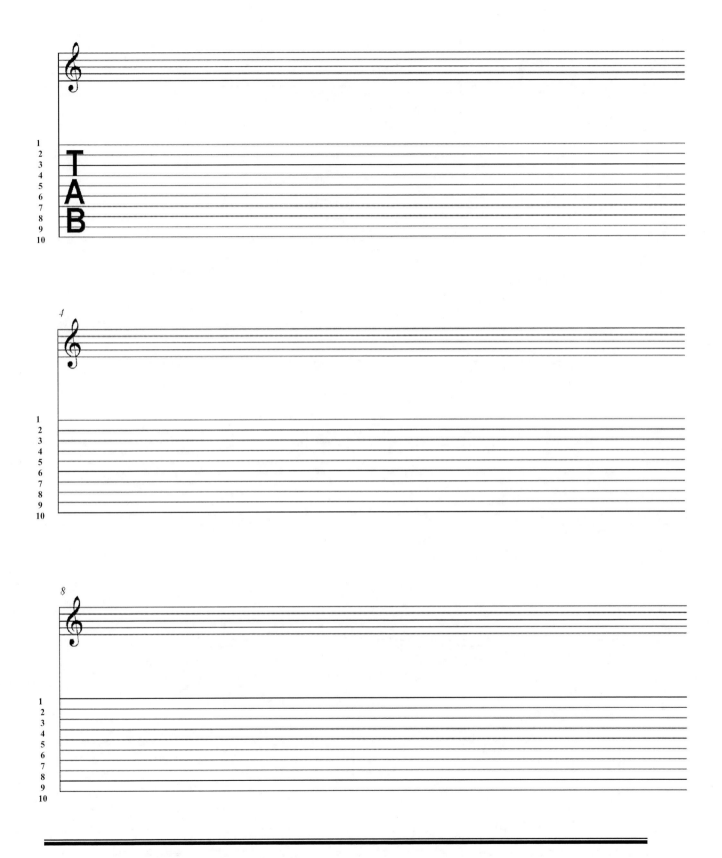

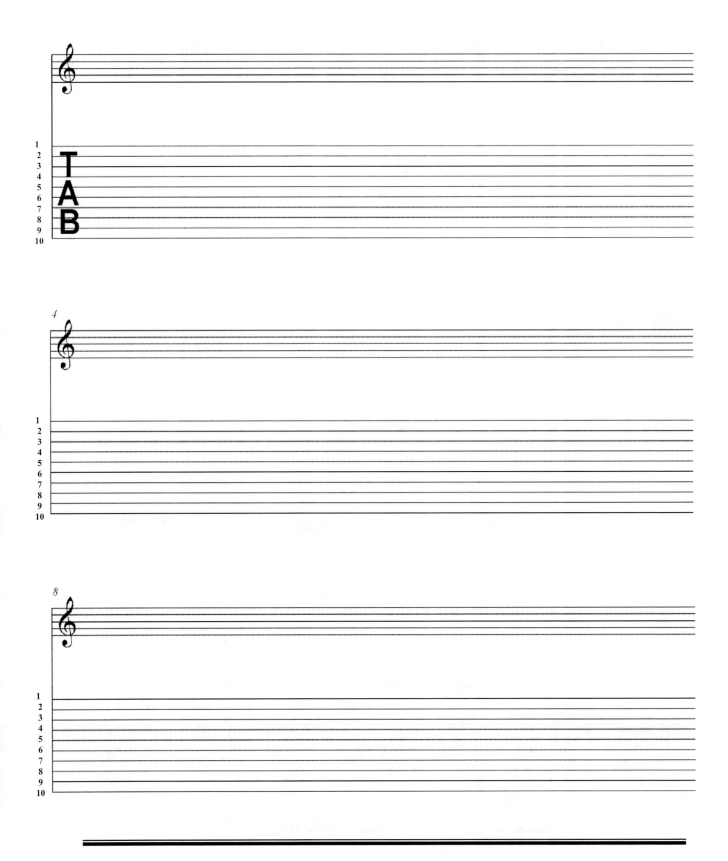

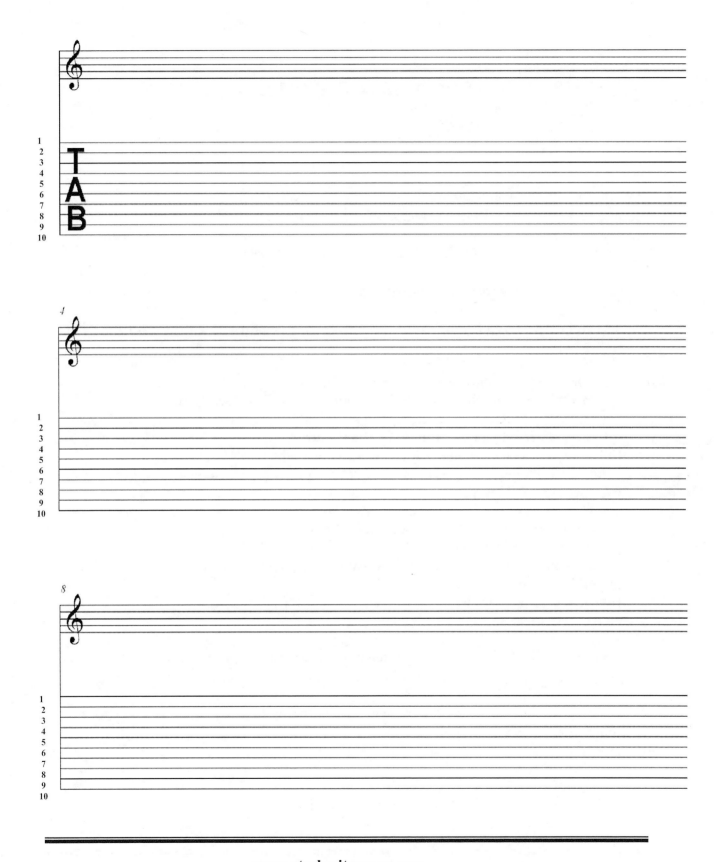

Steel Guitar Zone.com

Maximum Success Music Instruction

Thanks for purchasing the Pedal Steel Player's TAB Notebook.
Be sure to stop by **http://www.steelguitarzone.com** often to find new articles and products of interest to all pedal steel, lap steel and Dobro players including the best selling book and CD course ***Teach Yourself To Play Pedal Steel Guitar*** by Joe Stoebenau.

Some of the topics covered in this fantastic easy to use book:

- **The simplest, easy to use system of tablature ever presented! No more guessing what string to play.**
- How to make the classic pedal steel guitar sounds that will rip your heart out like a sharpened filet knife through a Louisiana Catfish!
- **The *easy* way to tune the pedal steel without being a rocket scientist.**
- How to make a melody sound vibrant and full by adding one note!
- **Easy to use even if you know nothing about music!**
- How to give a song an ending that will have them asking for more!
- **Why you don't need 17 knee levers to start out playing the pedal steel. (And what a knee lever is)**
- The secret to playing in tune you better know when playing with other musicians.
- **How to get more mileage out of your blues licks**
- Learn the scales you need to know without drinking 27 cups of coffee to stay awake.
- **Includes an audio CD with all the musical examples played slowly so you can learn them faster and easier!**
- How to play an entire song without moving your left hand!
- **And much, much more!**

Order your copy today at **http:www.steelguitarzone.com**

While you are visiting the website, be sure to sign up for my ***FREE*** daily Maximum Success Music Instruction Tips.